WHAT MAKES IT GO?

Written by Rod Barkman

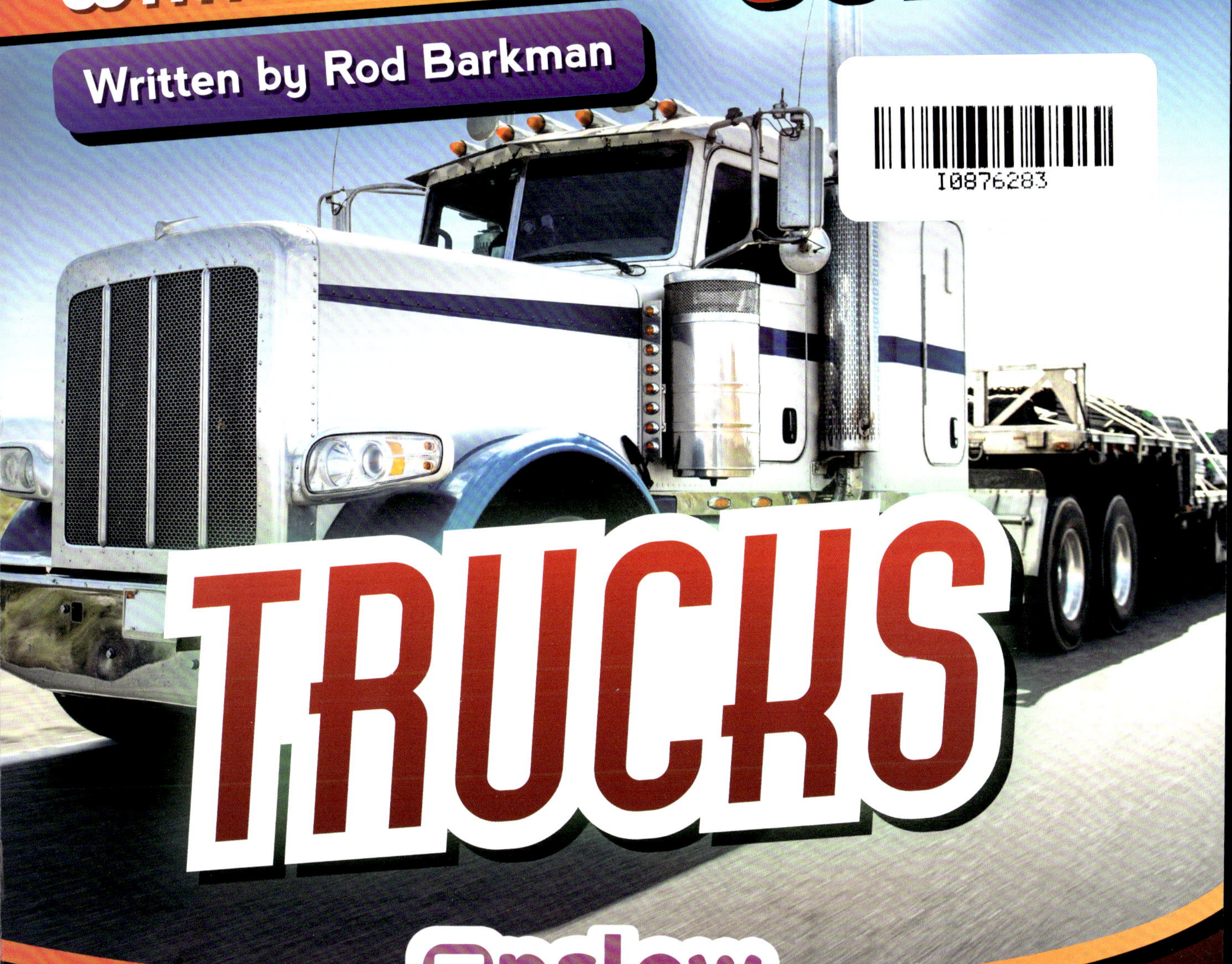

TRUCKS

Enslow PUBLISHING

Published in 2027 by Enslow Publishing, LLC
2544 Clinton Street
Buffalo, NY 14224

Written by: Rod Barkman
Edited by: Beth Latham
Designed by: Ian McMullen

Cataloging-in-Publication Data
Names: Barkman, Rod.
Title: Trucks / Rod Barkman.
Description: Buffalo, NY : Enslow Publishing, 2027. | Series: What makes it go? | Includes glossary and index.
Identifiers: ISBN 9781978548275 (pbk.) | ISBN 9781978548282 (library bound) | ISBN 9781978548299 (ebook)
Subjects: LCSH: Trucks--Juvenile literature.
Classification: LCC TL230.15 B375 2027 | DDC 629.224--dc23

Printed in China

CPSIA compliance information: Batch #QS27ENS: For further information contact Enslow Publishing LLC, New York, New York at 1-800-398-2504.

Please visit our website, www.enslowpublishing.com. For a free color catalog of all our high-quality books, call toll free 1-800-398-2504 or fax 1-877-980-4454.

Find us on

Image Credits

Images courtesy of Shutterstock.com, unless otherwise stated.

Cover and Recurring – Donglpix, Brandon Woyshni. 2–3 – Nigel Jarvis. 4–5 – Maksim Safaniuk, Virrage Images. 6–7 – Another77, phil_berry, F Armstrong Photography. 8–9 – NORRIE3699, Karolis Kavolelis, iampaese, yaalan. 10–11 – Mindscape studio, Virrage Images, Maksim Safaniuk, noina. 12–13 – creativecommons.org_Martin Dürrschnabel, David Buzzard. 14–15 – Scharfsinn, Vitpho. 16–17 – Phonpheth phiaphakdy, Zigmunds Dizgalvis. 18–19 – Canetti, CK Foto. 20–21 – CK Foto, AvokadoStudio. 22–23 – Scharfsinn, AlinStock.

CONTENTS

Page 4	What Is a Truck?
Page 6	Trucks in Everyday Life
Page 8	Types of Trucks
Page 10	What Is in a Truck?
Page 12	History
Page 14	How Do Engines Work?
Page 16	How Do Trucks Move?
Page 18	Trailers
Page 20	Safety
Page 22	The Future
Page 24	Glossary and Index

WORDS THAT LOOK LIKE THIS CAN BE FOUND IN THE GLOSSARY ON PAGE 24.

WHAT IS A TRUCK?

Trucks are vehicles that drive on land and have at least four wheels. Trucks often carry objects from place to place. They also do important jobs, such as helping put out fires.

Have you seen trucks like this on the road?

When objects are being taken from place to place, they are called freight or goods. Trucks carry goods, such as food or clothing, all over the world. The journeys they make can be very long.

The person who controls the truck is called the driver.

TRUCKS IN EVERYDAY LIFE

Bigger trucks can be specially built to carry certain things. A concrete mixer truck has a water tank and a drum that spins. This truck can bring ready-made concrete to a building site.

Dump trucks unload things like sand or gravel.

CONCRETE MIXER TRUCK

As well as carrying goods, trucks are used to save lives. Fire engines and some ambulances are types of trucks. They are specially built to help people in need.

TYPES OF TRUCKS

There are many kinds of trucks. How many of these have you seen?

Tractor trailers are large trucks that can typically carry a lot of heavy things.

Garbage trucks collect trash and take it away.

Pickup trucks are smaller trucks that are sometimes used by people who live and work in the country.

Monster trucks have big wheels and are driven in shows. Drivers perform jumps and tricks in monster trucks.

WHAT IS IN A TRUCK?

Different trucks are built to carry different things. A tanker truck is used to carry liquids, such as oil, milk, and water. Tanker trucks can carry gases too. These are kept in specially built tanks.

Refrigerated trucks often carry meat, fruit, vegetables, and frozen food. Just like a refrigerator, the truck is kept cold inside to stop the food from going bad. It has sensors that check the temperature.

REFRIGERATED TRUCK

This truck carries cars. It is called a car hauler.

HISTORY

The first truck powered by an engine was built in Germany in 1896. It was made by a man named Gottlieb Daimler. Two years later, a U.S. company made its own truck.

This is what the first trucks built by Daimler looked like.

In the 1900s, Americans built many roads all over the country. This made it easier for trucks to carry goods from city to city. Lots of trucking companies were set up to move goods around.

Today, trucks are an important part of moving freight around the United States.

HOW DO ENGINES WORK?

The engine of a truck works the same way as a car engine. However, a truck engine is much bigger and heavier. Most truck engines are powered by diesel, electricity, or gasoline.

TRUCK ENGINES ARE BUILT TO LAST AND HAVE MORE POWER TO MOVE HEAVY THINGS.

A truck engine powered by diesel has four stages.

1. Fuel comes in from the top as the piston moves down.

2. The piston moves up and the air and fuel are squeezed.

3. The air and fuel explode, knocking the piston down.

4. The piston bounces back up, pushing the burned gases out of the top.

HOW DO TRUCKS MOVE?

The engine is connected to a group of gears and rods. One of these rods is called a driveshaft. As the driveshaft spins, it turns the axles. On the end of each axle is a truck wheel.

As the axle spins, it turns the wheels, and the truck moves.

A small truck has two axles and therefore four wheels. Bigger trucks can have six axles, which means 12 wheels. More axles and wheels mean a truck can carry more weight.

TRAILERS

Some trucks are rigid, or fixed, meaning they are all in one piece. However, a tractor trailer has two pieces. The part that drives is called the tractor, and the part that holds goods is called the trailer.

The tractor and trailer are connected by a moving bar. This means the trailer can move around slightly, instead of being fixed in place. Tractor trailers are good at carrying heavier amounts over long distances.

SAFETY

Trucks have ways of keeping everyone safe. Many trucks use cameras to help the driver stay away from other vehicles or barriers. If the driver accidentally drifts too close, the truck steers itself away.

LANE MARKINGS

A truck can use cameras, sensors, and radar to see around it. Automatic brakes are turned on if the truck is moving too fast toward something and the driver doesn't brake. This can save lives.

Cruise control can help a driver stay at the right speed.

THE FUTURE

Trucks that use gasoline or diesel can harm the planet. Electric trucks aren't as bad, as long as the electricity comes from sources of renewable energy. In the future, many trucks will be electric.

The battery for an electric truck is charged at a charging station.

Trucks already have some ways to drive themselves and help the driver. However, in the future, trucks might not need drivers at all. Self-driving trucks use cameras and sensors to see what else is on the road.

Now you know a lot about trucks. What sort of truck can you imagine for the future?

GLOSSARY

diesel	a heavy oil that is used as fuel to make some engines work
drum	a cylinder-shaped container that is made to store things
gases	things that are like air, which fill any space available
gasoline	a light oil that is used as fuel to make some engines work
liquids	materials that flow, such as water
piston	a small, solid part of a machine that moves up and down
radar	a way of finding where something is by sending out radio waves, which are bounced back
renewable energy	power made from sources that do not run out, such as wind or solar energy
sensors	electronic devices that check something and react to changes

INDEX

cameras 20–21, 23
concrete 6
electricity 14, 22
engines 7, 12, 14–16
freight 5, 13
garbage 8
goods 5, 7–8, 13, 18
water 6, 10
wheels 4, 9, 16–17